Belsay Hall Garden and Castle

NORTHUMBERLAND

RICHARD HEWLINGS and STEPHEN ANDERTON

Belsay Castle, Belsay Hall and the garden are the nucleus of an estate that has belonged to the Middleton family since at least 1270. They lived in the castle until 1817, and from then until 1962 in Belsay Hall.

The fortified tower of the castle was built during a period of anarchy caused by Border Warfare between the fourteenth and sixteenth centuries. The unfortified range was added in 1614 as the unification of England and Scotland in 1603 had brought an era of relative peace.

The neo-Greek ornament of Belsay Hall and the exotic planting of the quarry garden are chararacteristic of the Romantic taste for primitive style and wild nature. The internal planning of the hall demonstrates the desire for comfort and informality of the early nineteenth century.

The landscape of the garden is of especial interest, with the formal garden by the hall blending into the wild woodland style of the quarries.

ENGLISH HERITAGE · LONDON

Contents

Published by English Heritage
23 Savile Row, London W1X 2HE
© *Copyright English Heritage 1994*
First published 1994, reprinted 1996, 2001
Printed in England by The White Dove Press Ltd
C50 1/01 FA6043
ISBN 1 85074 367 3

History

The terrace garden from a nineteenth-century watercolour

The Estate

Belsay Hall, the castle (which the hall replaced as the owners' principal home) and the gardens are the nucleus of an estate which was first recorded as belonging to a Middleton in 1270. Its owner at that time was the only member of the family to have become nationally prominent. He was Sir Richard de Middleton, Henry III's Lord Chancellor from 1269 until his death in 1272.

The family fell from eminence within one generation. In 1317 the Lord Chancellor's nephew, Gilbert, raised an army of men made desperate by the state the county had fallen into after Edward II's defeat at Bannockburn. They held to ransom two cardinals who were travelling to Scotland on a diplomatic mission, extorted a large sum from the Bishopric of Durham, and plundered southwards into Yorkshire, where the men deserted. Gilbert was captured and executed in London with his cousin John, the Lord Chancellor's heir. Belsay was forfeited and not returned to the Middletons until some time between 1371 and 1396. After that the estate was continuously occupied by

Belsay Castle in 1728, from an engraving by Samuel and Nathaniel Buck. The block on the left was demolished in 1872 but the walls of the main range stand to their full height and the tower remains intact

the Middleton family until 1962.

Since 1980 the nucleus of the estate has been in the care of first the Secretary of State for the Environment and then, from 1984, English Heritage. Around this nucleus lies a park which was created chiefly by Sir William Middleton, fifth baronet (1738-95), and Sir Charles Monck, sixth baronet (1779-1867). Around that again lies an estate which reached its present boundaries mainly in the seventeenth century. Sir Charles Monck and Sir Arthur Middleton, seventh baronet (1838-1933) were responsible for most of the physical evidence of this, in the form of farm buildings and houses. Sir Charles's wealth, and his eccentric personality, meant that he had more influence on the Belsay estate than any other member of the family. He extended the park to the south, demolished the old village of Belsay, which lay on the former road west of the castle, and built the present village on the Turnpike at Guidepost, to his own designs, between 1831 and 1860.

The park and estate remain the property of the Middleton family.

Belsay Castle

Until Christmas Day in 1817, when they moved to Belsay Hall, the principal seat of the Middleton family was Belsay Castle. The oldest part of this is the existing defensible tower of fourteenth-century type; it was certainly built by *c*1460 as wall paintings in the tower are heraldically connected with Sir John VI Middleton, who was active between 1439 and 1460.

An unfortified range, containing an ornamental entrance porch, was added to the left (west) of the tower by Thomas Middleton in 1614. To the left of this a large block, visually counterbalancing the tower, was added by Sir John Middleton, second baronet (1678-1717), probably in 1711 (see the illustration above).

Thomas Middleton was a tireless local justice and Puritan. In 1619-20 he served on a commission which indicted 358 recusants within the archdeaconry.

Twenty years later his religious zeal was less favoured. In 1639 he was in trouble for entertaining "unconformable ministers." In 1640 he was one of a group of local non-conformers who brought two leading Scottish Covenanters to Newcastle to show them the city's defences. The archbishop reported this in alarm to the Privy Council, adding "he has a private chapel at Belsay, where all comers are permitted to preach, to which the factious people of Northumberland have ordinary recourse when they are disposed to abandon common prayer in their parish churches."

Thomas supported Parliament in the Civil War, nevertheless his nephew and heir was created baronet in 1662. The first baronet maintained a Presbyterian minister at Belsay as domestic chaplain and tutor. Cumberbatch Leech, minister from 1698, was also the second baronet's steward and executor.

The castle lay to the north of a road running from east to west, of which the eastern part survives as the present drive. Sir William Middleton, fifth baronet, diverted this and other roads in the vicinity to extend his park, which eventually reached as far east as the Ponteland Turnpike (now the A696), at a point known as Guidepost.

Sir William's first two sons died in childhood and he was succeeded by his third son, Charles (1779-1867), when only sixteen. By the age of seventeen Charles had lost all his relatives except for two younger sisters, and, although a minor and a ward in Chancery, he had inherited estates in Northumberland, Essex and

Quarrying stone to build Belsay Hall from the site that is now the quarry garden

Drawing by Gertrude Middleton, August 1890

Lincolnshire. He was regarded as unusually careful in managing his estates, so in 1798 the Lord Chancellor appointed him receiver of his own property.

Sir Charles was obliged to take the name of Monck as a condition of his inheriting an estate in Lincolnshire from his maternal grandfather. Sir Arthur Monck (Sir Charles's grandson), the seventh baronet, resumed the name of Middleton in 1876.

Belsay Hall

Sir Charles built a new home, Belsay Hall, on a site south of the former road, between the castle and Guidepost. It was designed in 1806-07 (nearly 300 of his architectural drawings survive) on return from his honeymoon, which lasted from 11 September 1804 until 5 April 1806. He and Lady Monck were married at Doncaster. They travelled from Harwich to Husum in Denmark and then to Berlin, Dresden, Prague, Vienna, Trieste, Venice and Greece.

Sir Charles's design of Belsay Hall was greatly influenced by ancient Greek architecture. His diary and notes reveal that he was bewitched by the Romantic appeal of Greece. He attempted to marry the requirements of a modern country house to a resemblance of the ancient temple that he had most visited when in Athens, popularly (though not accurately) known as Theseion, or Temple of Theseus. The details and size of the columns and the proportion and outline of the building are those of Theseion.

The foundations, cut deep into the sandstone, were begun on 25 August 1807. Only in October 1809 was the masonry begun. On 27 September 1811 Lady Monck "walked immediately after breakfast to the new house and saw the first headstone put above a window." It was not until Christmas Day in 1817 that Sir Charles and his family moved in. Even then only the entrance hall and the bedroom above it were finished.

The stone from which the house was built was quarried within the park to the east of the site of the hall. When excavation was complete Sir Charles transformed the quarry into a Romantic garden, which is as vivid an expression of the horticultural enthusiasms of its age as Belsay Hall is of the architectural enthusiasms. It is these two features, in particular, which make Belsay so unforgettable.

Belsay Hall: Tour and Description

The entrance front of Belsay Hall showing the recessed porch (portico in antis)

Service side of the hall

Present-day visitors do not drive up to the main entrance of the hall. The one-storey ticket office (**1** on the illustration on the centre pages) was built in 1913 as a rear extension to the groom's cottage, which was within the stables. Beyond this the car park **2** lies in the angle formed by the west side of the stables and the north side of the hall. This was built of the same beautiful material as the rest of the hall: locally quarried stone. It was, however, felt that ornament was unnecessary as this was the service side of the hall.

The fourth storey is a mezzanine, unique to this side of the building. The other elevations appear to have only two storeys, but in fact they have a top storey, the windows of which all face a central light-well above the Pillar Hall.

The two-storey wing, projecting northwards, housed the kitchen until 1888 when Sir Arthur Middleton replaced it with a smaller kitchen within the main part of the hall.

In the summer refreshments can be bought in the old kitchen **3**.

The paddock, heated wall and gardeners' houses

On the other side of the car park the land drops down to a paddock (*not open to the public*) with, along the length of its far side, a raised bed against a heated wall **4**. This is probably the wall built in autumn 1832 and described by Sir Charles Monck in the *Horticultural Society's Transactions*. But there were earlier heated walls, as a payment to a "chimney sweep for Garden Wall" was made on 12 September 1807.

Heated walls, designed to protect fruit trees from frost, are thick enough to allow flues from an adjacent furnace to be formed horizontally within them. The heat would crack stone so Sir Charles had to introduce the discordant colour of brick. The furnaces were housed in lean-to sheds on the north side of the wall, and there are two other buildings attached to it.

To the right **5** is the gardener's house designed by Sir Charles in 1837 in the style of farmhouses seen by him in Italy for which Sir Charles's sketch, dated 1837, survives. To the left, is another gardener's house **6** first proposed in 1910. Both are now private houses.

Stables

The stables are approached from their rear and you see their interior before their main (south) elevation. The functions of the different rooms are known from one of Sir Charles Monck's drawings. The nearest room to the car park is the south room of the west wing, the former wash-house and now the shop.

From the shop **7** go up the stairs to the laundry. From here there is a door into what was intended as a hay chamber and a malt chamber; all three are now exhibition rooms. Stairs from the furthest room (the intended malt chamber) lead down to the open air.

Turn right (towards the ticket office), then right again into a north–south passageway. Before turning right yet again into the first stable, note the box on the left, which houses the suspension that still drives the stable clock, and, opposite it, the blocked fireplace, the flue of which was intended to heat two of the first-floor rooms. On both sides of the passage are lead downpipes to take rainwater off the roof.

Now go through the first door on the right of this passage. The purpose of the first room is not revealed on Sir Charles's drawing, but traces of four stalls of a similar type to those in the third stable survive on the floor and the walls. The present stalls are of the same type as those in the intended brewery (the next room), and evidently represent a rearrangement which also allowed the formation of the present door between the two rooms, dating presumably from the time when the intended brewery became a stable.

The second room, in the northeast corner, was intended to be a two-storey brewhouse, with convenient access to the malt chamber, but a first floor was inserted instead and, unlike the other upper floors, its underside was never plastered. The existence of open drains reveals that this, too, was used as a stable, at least from the date of the present paving. There is no trace of any earlier stalls or mangers, so the present ones may be the originals, but the inferior quality of their carpentry indicates that they housed inferior horses.

The last room is a stable which is below the hay chamber already visited. The stalls, zinc-lined troughs and mangers appear to be of Sir Charles's time, but the concrete engine footing and the printed labels are survivors of the house's occupation by the army in the Second World War.

The door in front of you, across the passage on the far side of the last stable,

The south front of the stables. On the left is the grassy mound that was the site of a chapel

leads into the former saddle room (*not accessible to the public*).

Turn left towards the front of the stable block **8**, off which the coach house opens. In it you can see the state coach of the High Sheriff of Northumberland. It was built by Atkinson and Philipson of Newcastle and is on loan from the Northumberland County Council.

The remaining rooms in the stable block are not open to the public.

On leaving the coach house, walk some 20 or 30 paces towards the hall then turn round. Only now will you see the principal elevation of the stable block, which was detailed to complement the hall. Its basic plan is traditional, with wings at each end and a central clock tower. The stable clock, inscribed "Paine. High St. Bloomsbury," is dated 1832.

In front of the stable block is a grassy mound **9** planted with trees. On the

Ordnance Survey of 1860 it is shown as the site of a chapel, and a map of 1784 shows there. Belsay, in the parish of Bolam, did not have a parish church. Instead, this may have been the Presbyterian chapel. It may have been abandoned when Sir Charles Monck conformed to the established church and the Presbyterian congregation moved to North Middleton.

BELSAY HALL
Exterior

Belsay Hall has two main storeys and an attic, hidden within a shallow hipped roof and facing inwards towards a central light-well. Its plan is a square of 100 feet (30m) with all the reception rooms opening off a two-storey hall below the light-well.

The principal reception rooms are on the south side, overlooking the terraces and with views of the rhododendron

The entrance front of Belsay Hall seen from the parkland

garden, the lake and Craig Heugh. The reception rooms are continued around the east and west sides in decreasing importance towards the north. The north side, already seen from the car park, is entirely functional and contains domestic offices which are separated from the Pillar Hall by a passage wide enough to contain

Capitals at the head of the columns in the Pillar Hall

secondary stairs. Thus, despite the biaxial symmetry of the basic plan, each side of the house has a different elevation.

The east side contains the entrance **10**. A traditional portico, standing proud of the main building, would have diminished the ancient Greek illusion that Sir Charles Monck wished to create (see page 6). He therefore designed a portico which is recessed in the main body of the building (a *portico in antis*). Visually this had the effect of intensifying the presence of the two prodigious columns; the light falls on them but leaves deep areas of shadow all round them; their size is exaggerated by the proximity of the enclosing walls, as if they were in a room. The traditional symbolism of columns, expressing authority (in this case of a baronet, a magistrate and a Member of Parliament) is clear, but not at the expense of the ancient temple image.

The south and west sides, where the family lived, are less formal. The Library, the principal room of the house, occupies the four central bays of the south front. The rooms at either end required more light than a strictly regular design would have given them. Sir Charles therefore doubled the size of their south-facing windows, dividing them by an unornamented stone mullion.

Entrance Hall

The portico leads into the entrance hall (**A** on the plan of the house on page 12). The Greek temple imagery is maintained by the unplastered walls of perfect ashlar masonry and a plaster ceiling imitating stone coffering. The two fireplaces replace niches, and are styled as temple doors.

The entrance hall divides the reception rooms (in front and to the left of you) from the domestic offices (to the right). Oak doors lead to the former; a green baize door to the latter.

Pillar Hall

The principal reception room is the top-lit Pillar Hall **B**, straight ahead (see page 13). Like the entrance hall, this is another room fashioned entirely in stone: floor, walls and even the ceiling of the colonnade and stairs. The capitals (ornamental heads) of its columns were put in place in 1812 and each was carved by a different mason. The balustrade, said to have been made from designs by Sir Charles's sister, was not inserted until 1830.

This room is surrounded by a two-storey colonnade housing a gallery on three sides; on the fourth side the stairs pass through the colonnade. The position of the colonnade creates a resemblance to the internal space of a Greek temple. Its ornament scrupulously follows Greek prototypes.

Like a medieval hall, the Pillar Hall was both a reception room and circulation area.

Dining Room, Library and Drawing Room

The three rooms designed exclusively for

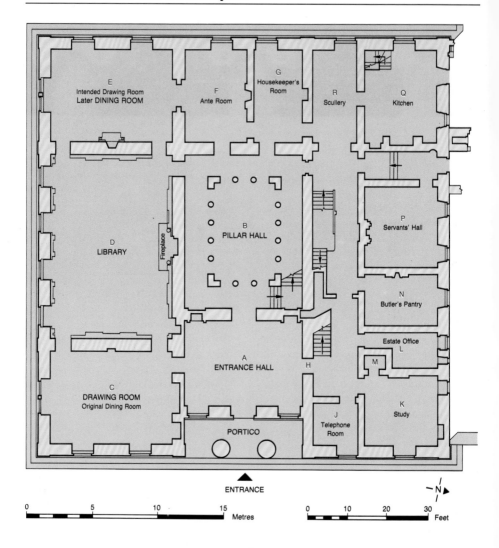

ENTRANCE

0	5	10	15
Metres

0	10	20	30
Feet

reception and family life lie on the south side of the house (to your left on entering). The Drawing Room or former Dining Room (**C**, entered from the entrance hall or from the Library) is in the southeast angle of the house. In 1909 it became Sir Arthur Middleton's study.

The Library (**D**, entered from the Pillar Hall or Drawing Room) is in the middle of the south side, and was in all but name

a drawing room also. It was the principal family room (see page 14).

The room **E** in the southwest (far left) angle was originally intended to be the Drawing Room but it remained a bare shell until 1909 when it was fitted up as the Dining Room. Only the former Dining Room **C** and the Library, therefore, were detailed by Sir Charles Monck.

Although Belsay Hall retains none of its

original furniture, old photographs reveal that it was comfortable and unostentatious. The house has less domestic technology than some houses of its period, but it has improved grates, shutters and double floors to reduce noise and heat loss. Sir Charles Monck's notebooks reveal his interest in central heating, smokeless grates and experimental lighting. Belsay Hall had plain but generous accommodation for servants.

The Pillar Hall in the 1930s

The Library in the 1930s. This was the main living room

Leave the Library and enter the later Dining Room **E**. Plans and one perspective drawing show that when this was proposed to be the Drawing Room an open colonnade was intended, separating it from the room at its north end. In 1909, when it was converted to the Dining Room, mahogany double doors were put into the north wall (all the doors of the primary period were oak), a wooden chimneypiece with fluted Doric columns was installed, and a fluted chair rail was applied to the wall, with, above it, a fluted wooden picture rail at low level and a brass one higher up. The numerous pictures which must have hung here were dispersed at auction in 1946 and 1962.

Next go to the ante room **F**. By looking

The next room to the north **G**, although finely finished in the primary period, became the Housekeeper's Room in 1887-88. This and the previous room now have no floors as these were infected by dry rot and removed in 1980. The voids have been left to show the structure of the house.

First floor
Now go upstairs and visit the bedrooms on the west and south sides. The first landing of the staircase has a fireplace, but Sir Charles's notes on carpeting the stairs indicate that this was originally a window to the entrance hall.

The arrangement of bedrooms has not been changed since Sir Charles's time, and most of the ornament of that period survives. All have identical *anthemion* (honeysuckle) friezes, except the central bedroom on the south side (the principal bedroom) which is slightly more elaborate. There are white marble chimneypieces in all rooms except the principal bedroom which has grey marble with white veins. The two rooms on the west side (i.e. nearest the top of the stairs) have contemporary grates but the others apparently have Edwardian replacements.

The joinery of the bed alcoves of the two smaller rooms in the south side is similar to the chimneypiece in the old Dining Room. The wallpapers, however, are all later. The blue flowered paper in the two west bedrooms is of a type produced in the 1880s, probably by Morris & Co, and may therefore be contemporary with the changes made to the office accommodation in 1887-88. The flowered paper in the west bedroom on the south side and the paper with classical ornament in the central bedroom appear to be later. The latter used motifs which were introduced by Robert Adam in the 1760s and revived at the very end of the nineteenth century. It is possible that

at the wall dividing this room from the Dining Room you can see that a wider opening between the two rooms was closed only at a secondary period. This was not a separate room until 1909. Had the proposed Drawing Room been created before then it would thus have been entered directly from the Pillar Hall as well as from the Library.

The Pillar Hall showing the stairs passing through the colonnade

this room was redecorated in 1909 as the window architraves have brackets similar to those of that date in the Dining Room.

The east bedroom on the south side is painted cream, but the cream overlies a grained paint finish simulating light-coloured oak wainscot, and it may be that the latter was the finish in Sir Charles's day.

Sir Charles Monck slept in the room in the northeast corner, allowing him to

Bedroom wallpaper from the 1880s

overlook the stables; Sir Arthur Middleton slept in the room in the southeast corner (*neither room is open to the public*). The latter room became John Middleton's when he succeeded to the estate on the death of Sir Arthur in 1933. Sir Arthur's eldest surviving son, Charles, who was John Middleton's uncle, became the eighth baronet but did not live at Belsay.

Sir Arthur's unmarried daughter, Elinor, a county Justice of the Peace, slept in the bedroom north of his on the east front. To the north of her, in the room overlooking the portico, Sir Stephen Middleton (the ninth baronet) slept as a child. Later he moved into the most easterly of the three bedrooms that are open to the public on the south side.

The room in the corner (*not open to the public*) was the Nursery, used by John, Stephen, and Lawrence Middleton when they came to live at Belsay on the death of their father, Commander Hugh Middleton, RN, in 1914. The room north of it on the west side was the Night Nursery. The room north of that was slept in by their mother.

Offices

Go back downstairs and enter the north range of the house through the baize-covered single door in the entrance hall **H**. These were the offices. When a telephone line was installed the room next to the portico became the telephone room **J**. The room in the northeast corner **K** was Sir Charles Monck's room of business. It and the room to its west **L** later became the Estate Office, and within them is a strong room **M**.

The room next to the Estate Office was the Butler's Pantry **N** and next to this was the Servants' Hall **P**. The use, in Sir Charles's time, of the rooms further west is not known, but in 1887-88 Sir Arthur ceased to use the kitchen in the north wing, and made the housekeeper's room in the northwest corner **Q** into a kitchen and the still-room immediately south of it into a scullery **R**.

Cellars

Stairs from the office passage descend to the cellars which are cut directly out of the bedrock. The cellars were begun on 25 August 1807, and were still potentially hazardous in October 1809, when a railing was put round them. There are four beer cellars and two wine cellars.

Other stairs lead to the surface in the north wing. The old kitchen **3** (*now a refreshment room in summer*) is straight ahead, and beyond that are a larder and an ornamental dairy. A door on the east side leads out to the car park.

To continue with the tour of the garden and castle, return to the entrance front of Belsay Hall **10**.

The Garden: Tour and Description

The view from the terrace, south to the rhododendron garden with Crag Wood and a glimpse of the lake beyond

The 30 acres (12ha) of garden open to the public today form the core of the nineteenth-century designed landscape made by Sir Charles Monck around Belsay Hall.

The site slopes gently westwards, at 400-50 feet (122-37m) above sea-level, and receives only 28 inches (71cm) of rain a year. The underlying rock is sandstone. Soils vary from a very sandy neutral loam overlying land-fill quarry waste on the terrace, to barely an inch or two of soil covering the levelled waste on the quarry floor.

All plants in the garden are labelled in Latin, and with a common name if one exits. A noticeboard with details of plants currently of special interest is on display in Belsay Hall.

A tour of the gardens commences at the front door of Belsay Hall **10** facing east across the park (see the illustration on the centre pages). The line of the old main drive can be seen running away across the field, past Lake Cottage. Of the parkland trees which remain, most are sycamore, oak and ash, with a large number of specimen thorns. On the lawns

18

South side of Belsay Hall from the lower terrace

surrounding the hall and stables grow the early flowering wild daffodil, *Narcissus pseudonarcissus*, and autumn-flowering *Crocus nudiflorus*.

The Terraces

Moving round to the south of the hall, you enter the upper terrace **11**, where simple close-mown grass reflects the austerity of Belsay Hall.

The lower terrace **12** follows as a complete contrast. The symmetrical, geometrical design of broad gravel paths, deep borders, and huge raised beds (or "pies") is planted with an informal medley of shrubs and perennials. Large and small mounded evergreens contrast their massed bulk with the looser or spikier forms of

Belsay Hall and stables, as seen from the southeast in the 1930s

COUNTRY LIFE

Rhododendron neriiflorum, from China, Tibet and Burma

herbaceous perennials, in the manner of a mixed border. Plants are allowed to spill generously out over the robust stone kerbs which edge all the beds.

Many of Sir Arthur Middleton's plantings from the turn of the century remain, including several large *Pieris floribunda*, *Magnolia* x *thompsoniana* and *M* x *weiseneri*, *Exochorda giraldii*, and *Osmanthus decorus*. The free-draining soil and southerly aspect allow the successful cultivation of more tender plants such as *Cistus*, *Halimiocistus*, and *Griselinia*, despite this being the windiest part of the garden. The terrace is also the flower garden at Belsay, where the traditional sights and smells of summer can be found.

In the central dissect-lozenge shape of stone-edged beds is a formal arrangement of hybrid musk roses ("Felicia" and "Moonlight"), *Yucca gloriosa*, *Hebe* "Mrs Winder," and an underplanting of headily scented old-fashioned pinks, such as the white "Mrs Sinkins." *Alchemilla mollis*, the native lady's mantle, is used as a cooler green foil.

Rhododendron Garden

The rhododendron garden **13** (*not open to the public*) forms the middle ground in the grandest of Belsay's views from the terrace. Most of the rhododendrons are hardy hybrids, planted between 1904-30. Many were planted very proudly, not as grafted specimens, but on their own roots. Consequently they have not been overwhelmed with suckers of *Rhododendron ponticum*, but remain largely as they were intended, red, pink, mauve and white hybrids. In the centre can be seen a number of old Ghent and Mollis hybrid azaleas. The main flowering period is from late May until mid June.

The low, rolling canopy of rhododendron foliage is punctuated by the crowns of birch, yew and laburnum, and the tall shapes of Lawson's cypress. The older cypresses are now coming to the end of their lives, but in the centre stand younger specimens from the 1950s.

Yew Garden

To the west, the terrace garden ends in an enclosure of yew hedges **14**. In 1980 the hedges were in poor health and much overgrown. They have since been gradually cut back to the trunks,

Magnolia x *weiseneri*

Magnolia x *thompsoniana*

commencing in 1986, and are forming dense formal hedges again, complete with their topiary finials. On the hedges grows the perennial South American nasturtium, *Tropaeolum speciosum*, with scarlet flowers and blue seeds.

The beds within the yew garden are treated formally also. Topiary cylinders of yew form the focus for areas of spring and summer bedding, while at the south end is a border of the autumn-flowering *Anemone x hybrida* "Alba," and *Hosta undulata*. At the north end grows the small white-flowered tree, *Hoheria glabrata*, under-planted with paeonies, *Hosta sieboldii elegans*, *Sedum spectabile*, and *Romneya coulteri*, the Californian tree poppy.

Magnolia Terrace

This broad walk **15** forms a link between the terrace and the winter garden **17**. It used to contain many summer-flowering species of magnolia, and these are now being replanted. They include *Magnolia sargentiana* "Robusta," *M salicifolia*, *M tripetala*, and *M virginiana*. At the east end stands a mature, 60 foot (18m) specimen of *Magnolia acuminata*, the cucumber tree. A screen of Portugal laurel, holly and evergreen oak closes the view out into the park.

Today only one side of the old parallel borders which used to flank the path remains. The border now contains plants from the turn of the century, from the postwar years, and more recent plantings. In the early season, *Viburnum farreri* and *V carlesii* are in flower, with another very large *Exochorda giraldii*. Through the summer, the general colour scheme is of pinks and purples. Shrub roses such as "Pink Grootendoorst," "Sarah van Fleet" and *Rosa glauca* and *willmottiae* rub shoulders with *Lavatera olbia* "Rosea," purple-leaved berberis, *Hydrangea* "Preziosa" and *Cotinus obovatus*.

Underplantings are allowed to spill out

Cistus x *cyprius*

on to the path, including *Phuopsis stylosa*, *Blechnum tabulare*, and *Geranium* "Russel Prichard." Taller herbaceous plants include the plume poppy (*Macleaya microcarpa*), *Eupatorium maculatum atropurpureum*, *Geranium psilostemon*, and the perennial white pea *Lathyrus* "White Pearl."

Above the magnolia terrace looms the woodland of Scots pine and Douglas fir underplanted with holly and yew. Belsay was known in the early nineteenth century for its collection of pines, and this dark woodland adjacent to the hall helps to lend the building an impression of its Mediterranean inspiration.

Around the summerhouse **16** grow

Camellia

The restored winter garden with azaleas in bloom

various species of Cistus, on the thin stony soil of the bank, while climbing roses flank its entrance.

Winter Garden

After the formality of the terraces, with their grand view across the valley, the winter garden **17** comes as something of a relief. It is a more social and less imposing space.

The focus of the winter garden is a pair of sunken croquet lawns **18**, which are regularly used.

To the west, the high sheltering wall is planted with many vigorous climbers such as *Vitis coignetiae*, *Vitis vinifera* "Purpurea," *Parthenocissus*, and many colour forms of *Clematis montana*. The wall is backed by the tall forms of the Nootka cypress (*Chamaecyparis nootkatensis*) and Western red cedar (*Thuja plicata*).

Above the east and north sides of the lawns, parallel borders flank the path. These borders have been twice replanted since the Second World War, lastly in 1984–85, but many of the original turn-of-the-century plants remain. There are some huge "dwarf" conifers such as *Chamaecyparis lawsoniana* "Nana" (12 feet/3.7m) and *Picea abies* "Clanbrassiliana," and old plants of *Rhododendron williamsianum* and *Buxus microphylla*.

Old photographs of the winter garden show quite tall, loose planting in these borders, and this is the style now being re-created, rather than the flatter, tighter look of more modern heather gardens. To this end, more tree heaths are being reintroduced, such as *Erica australis*, *E lusitanica* and *E terminalis*. The large plants of *Erica arborea* "Alpina" date from the early years of the century when the plant was introduced. This tree heath has the ability, unusual among heathers, to regenerate when cut down hard.

Contrast of foliage is provided by the use of plants with broader leaves, such as *Daphne retusa*, small rhododendrons, *Mahonia nervosa*, *Asarum europaeum*, and the Pacific coast irises.

Behind the borders is an evergreen backing of yew, variegated hollies, firs and pines. In the corner, the large 92 foot (28m) Douglas fir (*Pseudotsuga menziesii*) was planted in 1830, immediately after its introduction from North America in 1827.

The winter garden ends at a heavy door in the wall, overhung with a bower of flowering ivy. It marks the end of the formal half of the garden **19**.

Entrance to the Quarries

In contrast to the first half of the garden, the quarries represent a wilder, woodland style of gardening where the considerable work of maintenance is intended not to show. It is a man-made landscape, finished to look natural, then planted with exotic plants in such a way as to make them seem natural too.

Visitors are requested to keep strictly to the paths throughout the quarries.

On leaving the winter garden in early spring, there are snowdrops, double and

Hart's tongue fern

single, stretching away in all directions. On the right is the creamy trunk of an old specimen of the large-leaved birch, *Betula maximowicziana*, from Japan. Other species with ornamental bark are becoming established nearby. A large vine maple, *Acer circinatum*, is one of the first trees to show extravagant autumn colour. In the early summer grass grow bluebells, and many wild or naturalised cranesbills. The tiny pink and white *Montia sibirica* grows everywhere, even in the dry shade of beech trees.

Cornus kousa (Japanese dogwood)

The path leads on into the quarry, past a hedge of *Gaultheria shallon*. On the right, another hedge of ferns (male, lady and broad buckler ferns) is backed by trees and shrubs at the foot of the steadily rising rock face. They include the spiny *Aralia elata*, *Rosa moyesii*, with its long red hips, and the white-stemmed bramble, *Rubus cockburnianus*. Also here are *Acer sieboldianum* and *tschonoskii*, *Pieris formosa*, *Rhus verniciflua* (the varnish tree), *Corylopsis spicata*, and the cut-leaved elder. Beneath them grow *Phlomis russeliana*, *Persicaria campanulata*, *Centaurea macrocephala*, and the wild *Tulipa sylvestris*.

Meadow Garden

Passing through an iron gate, the path turns into the meadow garden **20**. This is the most open area of the quarries, lying between quarry face on one side and

1 Ticket office
2 Car park
3 Old kitchen
  Refreshment room in
  summer
4 Heated wall
5-6 Gardeners' houses
  (now private houses)
7 Shop
8 Front of stables block
9 Mound
  Site of chapel
10 Entrance to Belsay Hall
11 Upper terrace
12 Lower terrace
13 Rhododendron garden
  (not accessible to the
  public)
14 Yew garden
15 Magnolia terrace
16 Summer house
17 Winter garden
18 Croquet lawns
19 End of formal garden
  Door to quarries
20 Meadow garden
21 Great arch
22 Door in archway
23 End of quarry garden
24 West quarry

JAMES MORTIMER

The lines of the great arch are now softened by exotic planting in the cool shade of the quarry garden

mature woodland on the other.

At the turn of the century this glade, already remarked on as a flowering meadow, was fringed with exotic trees such as *Magnolia kobus* and *acuminata*, *Davidia involucrata vilmoriniana* (the handkerchief tree), *Cornus kousa* (the Japanese dogwood), and several *Parrotia persica* (the ironwood tree). These

ironwoods were bought from Veitch's nursery in 1911 for fifteen shillings each. There are also some older Japanese cedars around the meadow (*Cryptomeria japonica*).

In view of the fact that virtually no topsoil was imported, it was a brave move to try these trees here. They have grown slowly on this lean diet, and now in

The great arch

The meadow itself is mown after flowering and seeding, in August. A mixture of native and exotic wild flowers is naturalised in the turf. Cowslips and oxlips begin the season, followed by snakes-head fritillaries, single and double cuckoo-flowers, double creeping buttercup, pig-nut, sweet cicely, columbines, woodland cranesbill, *Camassia esculenta*, *Gladiolus byzantinus*, many colour forms of *Geranium pratense*, mints, and golden rod. In October the flowers of meadow saffron, *Colchicum autumnale*, and other hybrid forms, rise up through the short grass.

Under the rock face grow *Clematis flammula* and *rehderiana*, *Actinidia chinensis* (the kiwi fruit), *Garrya*, *Ribes menziesii*, *Staphyllea holocarpa* "Rosea," *Lilium pyrenaicum* and the blue, borage-like, evergreen alkanet (*Pentaglottis sempervirens*).

Quarry Garden

Passing under a grove of Japanese cedars, the quarry garden proper begins. There is cliff on both sides now, and the path runs westwards down this corridor of rock to the great arch **21** ahead, which links the two rock faces. The feeling of seclusion and the absence of wind is heightened by the line of yews and Scots pines which tower to 70 feet (21m) above the north cliff.

maturity are competing hard for the meagre food and moisture available on the quarry floor. In particular the fleshy rooted trees like Davidia and Magnolia find it a great struggle. Indeed the original handkerchief tree, planted about 1905, just four years after its introduction from China, died in 1990, from a combination of drought and honey fungus. A policy of regular and gentle mulching is helping to ensure the longevity of these remaining trees.

The quarry garden in spring

Below, on the stony quarry floor, grows a range of unusual trees and shrubs. There is *Enkianthus campanulatus* (from Veitch's nursery, 1908, for seven shillings and sixpence), *Quercus macrolepis* (the Vallonia oak), and a large *Eucryphia glutinosa*, with white flowers in August/ September, like single roses.

On the left, under the north-facing cliff, is a bank of native and exotic ferns, followed by a tall "doorway" into the grotto, perhaps the most contrived-looking piece of quarrying. Opposite, a small pond is fed from an underground water supply which also feeds the bog garden. Here the giant leaves of *Gunnera manicata* from South America rise up to 10 feet (3m) every year. In May the powerful scent of *Rhododendron fortunei* fills the air. Later the white, felted candles of new foliage on *Rhododendron rex* are especially striking. In a sheltered corner by the arch stands an old Chusan palm (*Trachycarpus fortunei*), its stem sheathed in the insulating layers of its old leaves, to protect it from the cold.

Beyond the great arch the quarry opens out into a second clearing ringed with cliffs and rock pinnacles. One pinnacle is covered with the autumn-colouring vine, *Vitis coignetiae*. Another is completely shrouded in flowering ivy, like a great evergreen tree.

In this sunnier more open space, rhododendrons up to 30 and 40 feet (9 and 12m) high flower in the early spring. *Rhododendron arboreum* "Roseum" begins to bloom as early as December in some years. *Rhododendron barbatum* and *R thomsonii* follow in March, then come *R campylocarpum, niveum, Loderi* "King George," "Cornish Cross," *brachycarpum* and many more. The season ends in July with the huge white scented trumpets of *Rhododendron auriculatum*.

The path now turns northwards past forms and hybrids of *Abutilon vitifolium*, and a small sunken cistern is overhung with the arching stems of the Chinese bamboo *Thamnocalamus spathaceus*.

In the narrowing rocky corridor stands an ancient *Pieris formosa* 35 feet (10.7m) high, and opposite is *Drimys winteri*, and

several plants of the delicate evergreen tree, *Azara microphylla*, the tiny yellow flowers of which fill the ravine with the scent of vanilla in spring.

Another tall archway of rusticated masonry and a heavy wooden door now block the path **22**. Beyond, a final gloomy corridor of stone only 8 feet (2.4m) wide leads on ahead. Trails of ivy hang low from the cliff tops and wood sorrel highlights the mossy ledges.

Finally the cliffs on either side subside and the path emerges from the hill into the sunlight again, under a bower of laburnum.

Belsay Castle

(*For full details see pages 4 and 41–7.*) As you emerge from the awesome gloom of the quarry garden **23**, the castle rises up to present a gentler romantic tableau. The castle sits comfortably in the parkland, separated from it only by a ha-ha. As at the hall, the bulk of the once-extensive

The quarry narrows

Belsay Castle

parkland planting has gone, but one monkey-puzzle tree (*Araucaria araucana*) remains south of the castle and dates from 1870 (see back cover). The oak below the east wall of the castle was planted in 1800 for Sir Charles Monck's coming of age.

When walking down to the castle, the shelter belt on the left includes a large Italian alder (*Alnus cordata*), more iron-woods (*Parrotia persica*), and two Californian redwoods (*Sequoia sempervirens*).

Around the castle there are massed informal plantings of snowdrops, daffodils, snowflakes (*Leucojum vernum*) and dog's tooth violets (*Erythronium dens-canis*).

Erythronium dens-canis
(dog's tooth violet)

In front of the part of castle to the left of the tower can be seen the remains of a late nineteenth-century formal garden, with stone-kerbed beds echoing the terrace gardens at the hall.

West Quarry

The return path from the castle follows a route through the later but equally large west quarry **24**. This second quarry is gardened very much as the first quarry garden may have been in its earliest years; it is a wild garden of native plants. Ferns clad the rock face and quarry floor,

The soft shield fern unfolds in spring, with a carpet of wood sorrel

baffling any hint of an echo.

In spring the ground lights up with the leaves of the tiny creeping *Saxifraga oppositifolia*. Snowdrops and primroses are everywhere. Honeysuckle hangs from the cliff-tops, and trees lean out from rock crevices in seeming defiance of gravity.

On the western cliff can be seen a semicircular hollow running up the face. This is the well shaft of the eighteenth-century kitchen garden, bisected by the quarrying.

Standing alone on the left in grass is a Wellingtonia tree (*Sequoiadendron giganteum*) from California.

Finally the path leads back past the meadow garden, where in autumn there are the wonderful colours of the red oak (*Quercus rubra*), ironwoods again, and the katsura tree (*Cercidiphyllum japonicum*). Set back to the right is an old Sitka spruce (*Picea sitchensis*), followed by a grove of tall Douglas firs planted in 1864.

You can return to the car park through the winter garden door, or through a wicket gate into the paddock. From this path, which passes under a group of walnut trees, may be glimpsed the long heated wall **4** (*not accessible to the public*) for the cultivation of peaches and nectarines.

Development of the Garden

Belsay Castle, watercolour by an unknown artist

Pre-1800

The parkland at Belsay slopes gently
upwards to higher ground at its western
edge. At this point, which commands
extensive views, there is an earthwork,
commonly referred to as a Roman camp,
but which is probably of slightly earlier
date, belonging to the Iron Age.

The site chosen for the castle was less
exposed, particularly from the prevailing
southwesterly winds, though it still held
wide command of the surrounding area.
The site of gardens or yards belonging to
the castle cannot now be made out, but
the medieval village settlement attracted
to the castle and manorial seat sprawled
along a main route leading from east to
west through the centre of the present
park, just south of the castle. Around and
to the north of the castle, the presence of
ridge-and-furrow preserved in the

grassland suggests that medieval open
fields once existed there.

After the castle was extended to the
west of the tower in 1614, more conscious
efforts were made to improve the setting.
Trees were planted in the parkland, and
during the early part of the seventeenth
century more substantial belts of
woodland were also planted along the
crags, including Bantam Wood to the west
of the castle, by Sir William Middleton,
third baronet. Snowdrops were planted in
the woods by his wife.

The engraving of Belsay Castle
produced by the Buck brothers in 1728
shows the Castle flanked and fronted by
formal gardens (see page 4). A pair of iron
gates opened out to the south and the
gardens were enclosed by walls and
railings.

Throughout the eighteenth century,

Archway of rusticated masonry. Beyond is a narrow corridor, quarried out of the rock

the parkland evolved around the castle, mainly under the impetus of Sir William Middleton, fifth baronet, between 1769 and 1795. His improvements included the building of Castle Bantam (the *ferme ornée*) west of the castle and the new serpentine drive from the north. This drive meandered through the park, presenting the grandeur of the castle in appropriate style. It crossed a newly formed lake by a new stone bridge. Many of these improvements were shown on an ambitious plan drawn up by Robson in 1792.

Sir Charles Monck, 1795–1867

The gardens as seen today at Belsay are a largely nineteenth-century creation. They represent a long period of continuous development from 1795 to 1933, made by only two men, Sir Charles Monck and his grandson Sir Arthur Middleton.

In 1807, when the building of Belsay Hall began, the focus of the parklands moved east from the castle to the hall. It

was a time of great changes in landscape style and fashion. The eighteenth-century landscape park of sixty years before, epitomised by the work of "Capability"

The garden (south) front of Belsay Hall. The massive arcaded ha-ha supports the lower terrace; it is reminiscent of Repton's design for Michel Grove (see page 34)

Repton's drawing of Michel Grove Sussex

Brown, was beginning to be considered too insipid and artificial for the taste of the day. This reaction in favour of wilder more natural landscapes aimed much of its criticism at Humphry Repton, Brown's successor as the nation's leading landscape designer. The new movement became known as the Picturesque movement, because it advocated the creation of such craggy landscapes as appeared in the paintings of Claude and Poussin.

Sir Charles's new landscape and garden at Belsay were made broadly in the Picturesque style, but with clear debts to both Brown and Repton. The garden was modern and forward looking, like the hall itself.

To make way for the new hall and garden, the medieval village and chapel were swept away, and the castle was greatly reduced. A new village, well out of sight, was built to the east of the hall and castle. In between, Sir Charles planned to extend Belsay Lough to form a substantial lake, but after vociferous complaints from newly settled villagers it was never flooded. Instead, a new lake was made to the south of the hall.

Belsay Hall faces east into the park, where Sir Charles planted trees, not in the belts and clumps of Brown's manner but in random groupings of individual trees. Two cartloads of stone were used, laid on edge, to protect and secure each tree. The arrangement of the trees was such that visitors arriving at the hall would not see the building until relatively late. By creating a ha-ha and sunken drives in front of the hall, it was made to appear as if the grass park swept right up to the door of the hall in the eighteenth-century style. The stable block was sited to protect the hall from cold northeasterly winds. The remains of the medieval chapel, now covered in birch trees and ivy, separated the hall from the stables.

The garden front of the hall looks south over two deep terraces and commands the view of the valley below like a temple in an Arcadian landscape painting. Sir Charles's gravel drive ran right along this upper terrace to the steps at the west end. The lower terrace is supported by a massive arcaded ha-ha, reminiscent of Repton's design for Michel Grove (see opposite page). On this terrace Sir Charles made the simple geometric stone-kerbed beds which look forward in style to the more complex parterres of the High Victorian period. These beds were probably informally planted at first and later filled with bedding plants. The paths were made of sand.

The view south from the hall was Sir Charles's most ambitious piece of landscaping. The steep, rocky hillside opposite was planted with a mixture of newly introduced exotic conifers, Scots pines, and native hardwoods, to form a sombre backdrop to the new lake with its little cascade. On the middle ground, a two-acre hillock covered in broom, Sir

Charles experimented with growing monkey-puzzle trees (*Araucaria araucana*). Flanking and framing this view were more parkland trees. The rough broken terrain and brooding north-facing water were a far cry from the close-grazed serenity of a Capability Brown lake shore.

Immediately west of the hall Sir Charles planted a wood of Scots pines and Douglas fir (*Pseudotsuga menziesii*). Below this, the grass terrace swept westwards, the path flanked by parallel borders of brightly coloured annuals, overlooking parkland, and stopping finally where the Winter Garden ends today. This marked the end of the formal half of Sir Charles's garden.

There then began the walk through the quarry, Sir Charles's most remarkable essay in the Picturesque style. Although the medieval village had been razed to the ground, to improve the prospect of the castle and make way for the quarry itself, Sir Charles kept the last house of the

A late nineteenth-century photograph of the castle

The quarry by J Liddell

village, Townfoot, which stood beside the track at this eastern entrance to the quarry. This was the last sign of Man, as it were, a simple rustic abode, before one plunged into the awesome rocky landscape of the quarry.

The quarry itself was excavated with very great care to leave a Picturesque canyon which cuts through the hill, connecting the hall and castle in a great L-shape. The towering cliffs, pinnacles and rock arches were intended to make the human visitor seem small, to feel the thrill of the Sublime, as one might from a painting of Salvator Rosa. To enhance this effect, yews and pines were planted in a line almost a quarter of a mile (400m) long on the northern cliff top. Yet at the same time this was the garden of a Georgian gentleman and his family, so the path through the quarry was made easy, level going, with what Repton called "the comfort of a gravel path."

Planting in the quarry was strictly limited, and certainly no soil ever seems to have been introduced. The Picturesque ideal allowed for fewer and fewer exotic plants the further one strayed from a house towards the wilder "natural" landscape. So here, rock was everything, with a few native trees. It is interesting to compare the fantastic landscape paintings of John Martin, or the stage designs of Philip de Loutherbourg, with contemporary drawings of the quarry at Belsay. Even so, Sir Charles, like all keen gardeners, was affected by the thrill of new plants, and by 1852 he was experimenting in the quarry with such exotic new rarities as the Chusan palm (*Trachycarpus fortunei*) and *Fitzroya cupressoides*. He also showed interest in the variety of wild flowers and native ferns to be found in the quarry.

At the castle Sir Charles undertook major alterations to make the buildings fit in with his Picturesque scheme. The castle was reduced almost to its seventeenth-century proportions, while ruined parts of the eighteenth-century house were left covered in creepers or ivy. The formal gardens and walls in front of the castle were swept away, and the landform considerably altered to disguise the previously level site. A ha-ha was made to the south and east so that, to visitors emerging from the quarry, the castle appeared to sit directly in the parkland. The parklands around the castle were extensively replanted, to enhance the view and give shelter to the quarry.

Sir Charles's garden at Belsay, then, was one of linear progression, based upon the contrast between the ordered, civilised, and exotic plantings around the hall, and the wilder "natural" quarry and crag woods. But any picture of Sir Charles's garden must also make room for

The great arch
by J Liddell

COUNTRY LIFE

The quarry garden and great arch in the 1930s

his up-to-date kitchen gardens, and his great interest in growing fruit on the heated wall (see page 8).

Sir Arthur Middleton, 1867–1933

Sir Arthur Middleton's period of influence on the gardens may be seen as an elaboration and enrichment of the structure laid down by Sir Charles Monck. Sir Arthur undertook no undoing of his grandfather's work anywhere, although he did extend the garden in part, and made alterations to the style.

Sir Arthur seems to have had no great attachment to High Victorian gardening, at the hall at least. But, more than Sir Charles, he did have the passion for growing and collecting new plants, like so many other nineteenth-century garden owners.

This was the time of the great plant introductions, and new species of plants of all kinds were coming into the country from abroad. The face of English gardens, from whatever preceding period, was

changing rapidly. Sir Arthur made full use of these new plants, and notably of rhododendrons, to embellish with colour the restrained cartoon of Sir Charles's Picturesque landscape. He also was influenced by the writings of the late nineteenth-century gardening writer William Robinson, who advocated the naturalising of exotic perennials, while attacking the crudities of Victorian formal gardening.

These combined influences led Sir Arthur to change the garden he had inherited, towards a looser, more informal, planting in the formal part of the garden, and a more colourful, exotic, planting in the informal part. The result was to blur and soften the previous sharp distinction between the two parts of the garden. Most significantly, the softening and relaxing of the planting on the terrace garden, from its sharper, brighter, geometric beginnings, has left the hall looking even more uncompromisingly stark in its setting.

On the upper terrace, south of the hall, Sir Arthur removed the gravel drive and put it down to grass. A metal fence and gates were put in, making the terrace a separate entity from the park sweeping up to the hall on the east. The upper terrace walls were also lowered to make the view to the south less restricted from indoors. The vigour and grandeur of Sir Charles's design was being broken down into more intimate spaces.

On the lower terrace, Sir Arthur replanted the beds at the turn of the century, with a mixture of shrubs, climbers, perennials and low-growing evergreens, which was well documented by Christopher Hussey in *Country Life,* October 1940.

Across the valley, on the middle ground before the lake, Sir Arthur massed Hardy Hybrid rhododendrons, in the years especially from 1903-14. The Lawson cypresses (*Chamaecyparis lawsoniana* "Erecta Viridis," etc) here date from the second half of the nineteenth century.

The terrace was further subdivided in 1897 when the small garden enclosed by yew hedges was planted. A second hedge of Lawson cypresses was planted to shelter the young yews, but never taken out as intended.

On the magnolia terrace summer-flowering species of magnolia were collected, and behind Sir Charles's parallel borders beside the path, island beds were made in the lawn, to grow Mollis azaleas. On the edge of the wood above, the summerhouse was erected.

The winter garden was a development entirely of Sir Arthur's. Where previously Sir Charles's L-shaped parallel borders had simply overlooked parkland, Sir Arthur removed the trees and levelled up the land to form croquet lawns and a tennis court.

To the south the view remained into the park. To the west he built a high wall of possible Florentine inspiration, backed by ranks of dark Nootka cypresses (*Chamaetyparis nootkatensis*, planted 1875) and Western red cedar (*Thuja plicata*). In the borders were planted low evergreens, heathers, and dwarf conifers, backed by taller evergreens and hollies.

Sir Arthur's main contribution to the quarry as he found it was the introduction of trees, shrubs and climbers, and in particular species rhododendrons. Perennials were naturalised in the grass, colonising the quarry floor, and deciduous flowering trees were planted around the meadow. This was the smartest, most gardenesque, phase in the quarry's development.

The pond and the second arch with its wooden door also belong to Sir Arthur's period of gardening.

Around the castle Sir Arthur planted more ornamental trees, and in front of it a fussy garden in a typical late nineteenth-century manner. It is not clear, however, whether this development was Sir Arthur's or that of the occupying estate steward.

During the whole of Sir Arthur's tenure, quarrying took place alongside Sir Charles's quarry (the quarry garden), and stone was being extracted in a small way even until the 1930s. Whatever Sir Arthur's intentions for this second ring of quarrying may have been, he certainly worked the stone in the same style as Sir Charles had done, making another L-shaped canyon, now wide, now narrow, with wings of rock projecting from either side to break the quarry into compart-ments. This quarry cut through the site of the old eighteenth-century kitchen garden, which had served the castle until the building of the hall.

Much of Sir Arthur's interest in perennials and low evergreens such as heathers came from reasons of economy. He greatly reduced the amount of energy devoted to the kitchen gardens at Belsay, and had abandoned the use of the heated wall before 1895.

Postwar years

During the Second World War Belsay was in military hands and the gardens were untended. After the war, a new garden staff was appointed by Sir Stephen Middleton and some replanting took place within the garden. The replanting of parkland trees had largely stopped with the First World War.

In the 1950s the garden was briefly open to the public. The last gardener, Mr James Holms, retired in 1973, and the garden again stood still until the physical work of restoration began under the Department of the Environment in 1982.

Restoration

The initial thrust of the restoration work took place between 1982-84, under the guidance of consultant landscape architect Mrs Elizabeth Banks, of Land Use Consultants, London. The main contractor for the work was Sones Landscapes of County Durham, under Clerk of Works, Miss Jane Furse. The finer tuning of the project continues today.

The aim has been to restore the formal garden to its appearance in the 1920s and 1930s. In the quarries and the informal half of the garden, the plantings made by Sir Arthur Middleton at the turn of the century have now passed beyond their tidy gardenesque youth and are as old and Picturesque as their landscape setting. In the quarry garden the aim is to maintain a wild Picturesque effect, but using exotic plants, while the west quarry will continue to house purely native plants, to show the style of the quarry garden before the introduction of exotic plants.

At the castle no plants remain from the late nineteenth-century garden and, as the quarry garden is now near to its original Picturesque intentions, the castle will not be gardened again. Rather it serves as the simple Picturesque ruin to end the quarry walk, much as it did in Sir Charles's time when the hall was new.

Belsay Castle before the western block was demolished, drawn by Edward Swinburne in 1819

Belsay Castle: Tour and Description

Belsay Castle today. This is a good point from which to view the castle as it shows the remains of the block on the left, which once balanced the main range and the tower

Castle exterior

You emerge from the quarry garden southwest of Belsay Castle. The distant view allows its component parts to be identified: the defensible tower, the unfortified two-storey range with an ornamental porch and, to the left (west), the remains of a three-storey block which visually counterbalanced the tower (see the illustration on page 4); behind the tower is a two-storey office range.

From this viewpoint you will best appreciate that the tower was designed both for defence and for display. It is of fourteenth-century style and was certainly built by *c*1460 (see page 4). Also from this point, but across the fields to the left and not accessible to the public, you can see

Castle Bantam, a folly which once had a spire and some limited accommodation.

Until 1784 a road ran just south of the castle, from east to west, following the line of the existing main drive, and continuing across the meadow past the point where you emerged from the Quarry Garden. Thus visitors today get their first clear view of the castle from the vantage point intended since the fourteenth century, as the principal decorative features of the tower are on the south side where they could be seen by travellers. These include the higher turret in the southwest corner, the ornamental first-floor windows, and the moulding around the crenellations, which is continued around both vertical and horizontal edges; on the other sides

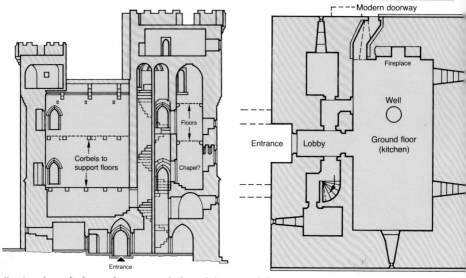

Section through the castle tower and plan of the ground floor

this moulding is limited to the horizontal edges.

For security the ground floor is lit by little more than slits; the parapet is crenellated (it has alternating heights to allow defenders either to lean out or to take shelter) and machicolated (it projects and has holes in the floor of the projection to allow hostile material to be dropped on attackers). It is possible to examine these defensive features from the roof of the tower.

The tower also has two larger and ornamental windows on the first floor, both of them mullioned (divided by vertical bars of stone) and one of them also transomed (divided by a horizontal bar) and ornamented by geometrical patterns sunk into the single stone which forms its tympanum (the triangle with curved sides above the lintel).

The roofline features are not exclusively functional: the projecting circular corner turrets, the crenellation and machicolation are intended to give the impression of strength and advertise the independence of the lord as much as to actually repel his enemies.

On the far left is all that remains of the west wing, which was probably built in

The porch and partly blocked original doorway to the main range

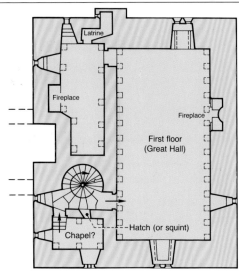

Plan of the first floor of the castle tower

1711. In the middle is the main range with its central two-storey porch of 1614. The part of the main range on the left of the porch was completely rebuilt in 1872 for Sir Arthur Monck by Ross and Lamb of Darlington as a compact modern house; the part on the right was just refaced. All but part of the walls of the west block was demolished.

Walk down towards the west end of the castle and then along its south front. The porch has the owner's achievement of arms (the legal sign of his position) carved in stone over the door, with the proclamation: THOMAS MIDDLETON AND DORATHY HIS WIFE BVILDED THIS HOVSE ANNO 1614.

The doorway in the porch was closed in the nineteenth century. Since 1872, if not before, entry has been by a door just left of the porch. This leads into what was the main hall of the Ross and Lamb house. In front of you was a staircase, as can be seen from the impressions on the wall. A rear porch survives on the north side.

To the west (left) was the 1872 drawing room (*not accessible to visitors*) which had a bedroom and a maid's room above. The room to the east (right) of the present entrance may stand on the site of the 1614 great hall and perhaps an earlier one. The surviving grate, oven and boiler show that in the nineteenth century one of these rooms had become a kitchen.

On Christmas Day in 1817 the family moved out. A picture dated 1819 shows the castle still intact. By 1843 another view shows the west wing ruinous. At some time before 1858 the castle became the steward's accommodation. In 1897 the tower was repaired and reroofed. By 1980, when the castle came into guardianship, the roof of the main range had collapsed.

THE TOWER: ground floor
Steps lead down to an arched doorway to the tower. It can be debated whether the tower was initially free-standing and had the main range added on its west side, or whether it was itself added at the east end of an earlier main range. If the former,

The impressive battlements of Belsay Castle

this doorway would originally have been external, defended by two projections or short wings either side of it.

Above this doorway is a blocked doorway and above that, at second-floor level and now obscured by a later chimney, is another door which does not have any indication of having been added after the tower was built. If the tower was originally free standing, these doors, the higher of which opens out of the most private chamber, could either have led on to ornamental galleries, or operated some sort of defensive device at high level. On the other hand, if the tower was an addition, these doors would have led either into the first and second floors of the main range or on to its roof.

The ground-floor doorway leads into a barrel-vaulted lobby with three similar doorways opening off it. The doorway to the left (north) leads into another lobby, perhaps a porter's lodge or kitchen office

as it has access to the kitchen; opening off this little room is an unlit room, presumably a store or strong room. The door ahead leads into the principal ground-floor room, a pointed barrel-vaulted room with a well, now sealed off but formerly 17ft (5m) deep, near its north end and a huge fireplace (now partly filled in) in its north wall, which identify it as a kitchen.

The stone newel staircase (a spiral staircase radiating from a central newel post) is south of the entrance lobby. South of the stairs is a stack of closets (the first, second and fifth are vaulted), four opening off the stairs (the first on the ground floor).

The stairs reach the third closet at a point higher than its floor level, so it is entered by steps down from the stairs. This closet has an opening like a window between its doorway and the doorway to the Great Hall. Sir Arthur Middleton believed this to be a squint, with a view of an altar within the closet, and thus that the closet, which has an ornamental south window, was a tiny chapel. Alternatively it has been argued that the opening was not a squint (because its awkward position on the stairs would have permitted only one person at a time to see the altar) but a serving hatch for taking food from a kitchen to the Great Hall (see the plan on the right, page 43). As it had no fireplace and no direct supply of water, it seems likely that this closet was not itself a kitchen, but a dresser where meals that had been cooked on the ground floor were arranged and ornamented before being passed through the hatch and formally taken into the Great Hall. The reason for the ornamental window in the south wall may well be as explained on page 41.

The Tower: first floor

The doorway beside the hatch leads into the large room over the kitchen. Although it no longer has a ceiling, a row of corbels (squared stones projecting from the wall) can be seen which formerly supported the beams of the floor above.

This first-floor room was evidently the most important in the tower; the room above was probably the next most important. The first-floor room was heated by a fireplace ornamented by an arched lintel. It was lit by the two most ornamented windows in the tower, one at each end, and both with straight-sided round-arched reveals, wide enough to accommodate two stone window seats. Activities requiring good light, such as needlework, reading or writing, could have been carried out on these seats. At night heat was conserved by closing the wooden shutters, the bolts of which were shot into bosses in the mullions which can still be seen.

At the south end of the east wall is an unornamented window. Its position might be explicable had the room been

subdivided by a partition which in medieval houses was called the screens; its height might be explained if it lit a music gallery.

There is a doorway with an arched lintel on the west side of the room at the north end (see Chambers, below). Its threshold is higher than the floor of the room, as is the floor of the northern window recess. This suggests that the floor at this end of the room was once higher, like a platform or low stage; in medieval houses or the great halls of castles this was known as a dais.

Large rooms with more ornament than most, a screens passage at the entry end and a dais at the other end were called halls in medieval times, and were the principal room of assembly. Twice a day the household would assemble there to eat, and at other times visitors would be received there, formal business would be conducted, and justice would be administered.

The grate, oven and boiler show that this room became a kitchen after the doorway was made into a window. Note the first-floor fireplace above

The Great Hall in the tower. Note the projecting stone corbels, which supported the floor of the first-floor Solar, and the stone window seats

The room is distinguished by a rare survival: part of the painted plaster decoration which at one time may have adorned all its walls. Although very decayed, it can still be seen on the south wall and on the underside of the arch of the south window. It includes a dark red vine trellis pattern, tree trunks with neatly sawn-off branches from which shields have been hung, ships with masts and sails but not rudders, and smaller boats being paddled rather than rowed. The heraldry indicates that this is the work of Sir John VI Middleton, who lived in the first half of the fifteenth century.

The Tower: second floor

The now-floorless room above was similar but less highly ornamented. Its two ornamented windows have mullions but no transoms, and its fireplace has a straight lintel. This may mean that the room's use was similar to that of the hall but less important; or that it was a room for the private use of the family, and that they decorated it more intimately, but perhaps more richly, with hangings rather than wall paintings. It could have been a Solar (a private withdrawing room of the lord) or a great chamber, where he and his family or friends dined privately while the rest of the household dined below.

Chambers (bedrooms)

The two rooms, one above the other, opening off the west side of the north end of the Hall and Solar are the most luxuriously appointed of the tower. The lower room has a window facing west and both have a window to the north, beside a latrine, and a fireplace in the west wall. As the Solar has no floor, only the lower chamber is now accessible.

These were evidently chambers for the two most important members of the household, perhaps the lord and his heir, or the lord and his constable (castle keeper). The upper chamber has the blocked door, mentioned on page 44, in its west wall, once leading out to a gallery (either for pleasure or defence) or on to the roof of the adjoining range.

Roof of the Tower
From the Great Hall continue up the newel stairs to the roof of the tower, past the closets in the south side – two with no floor, others with a stone floor over the closet below. At the top of the stairs, look up at the fine eight-ribbed vault.

N.B. When on the roof please keep to the walkways and keep children under control.

From the roof you can look at the machicolations on the east and west sides. The chimney was added in 1872.

Three corner turrets each contain a vaulted closet, lit by a loop (a vertical slit which could be used by an archer), but the higher southwest turret contains two closets; the upper one could be heated and therefore was of higher status. This upper closet is the top of the stack to the south of the newel stairs. Unlike the lower closets, it is not reached from the stairs, but by steps from the roof. It is twice the size of the lower closets as it extends over the vault at the top of the stairs.

The Castle Offices
Return to the kitchen on the ground floor and leave the building by the door to the left of the fireplace. This door cannot be original as it exits almost at the bottom of a huge shute from the latrines in the two chambers. To the left of this door there is a two-storey wing running two

Eight-ribbed vaulting above the newel staircase in the tower

COUNTRY LIFE

chambers. To the left of this door there is a two-storey wing running northwards; it was not linked to the tower until the nineteenth century. This wing has similar masonry to the tower and may also be medieval.

At the far end of this wing is the office court of Belsay Castle. Along its west side is a fine range of eighteenth-century stables, perhaps the hunters' stable which was slated in 1769. Kennels on the east side of the court were designed by Sir Charles Monck.

At the far end of the court there is a gate with a view across the park to an ornamental building called Castle Bantham. The exact date of this building is uncertain but it was in existence by 1769 and in 1771 a man was hired to live in it. The detailing is Gothick, with a crenellated parapet, and a quatrefoil (shape like four leaves) opening to a pigeon loft.

To return to Belsay Hall or the car park, start back the way you came but turn right into the West Quarry (see page 31).

Bibliography

The chief source of information is the Middleton family papers, on loan to the Northumberland Record office, Meldon Park, Gosforth, Newcastle upon Tyne.

LOCAL HISTORY
L E O Charlton [editor], *Recollections of a Northumbrian Lady, 1815 to 1866*, 1949, 200.
A H Page, *Whose Light Must Never Die*, 1962.
Anthony Tuck, *Border Warfare*, 1979.
S J Watts, *From Border to Middle Shire: Northumberland 1586-1625*, 1975, 82, 152, 156, 199.

LOCAL ARCHITECTURE
Mark Girouard, "Dobson's Northumbrian Houses," *Country Life*, 17 and 24 February 1966, 352-6, 406-9.
Tom Faulkner and Andrew Greg, *John Dobson Newcastle Architect 1787-1865*, 1987.
Peter Ryder, "Fortified Buildings," in John Grundy, Grace McCombie, Peter Ryder, Humphry Welfare and Nikolaus Pevsner, *The Buildings of England Northumberland*, 1992, 58-67.

EARLY NINETEENTH-CENTURY ARCHITECTURE
Nikolaus Pevsner, "The Doric Revival," in *Studies in Art, Architecture and Design*, I, 1968, 197-211.
John Summerson, *Architecture in Britain 1530 to 1830*, 1953, 269-321.
Henry-Russell Hitchcock, *Architecture, Nineteenth and Twentieth Centuries*, 1958, 59-76.
David Watkin, *Thomas Hope 1769-1831 and the Neo-Classical Idea*, 1968.
J M Crook, *The Greek Revival*, 1972.
Mark Girouard, *Life in the English Country House*, 1978, 213-44.

MIDDLETON FAMILY
John Hodgson, *History of Northumberland*, part II, volume I, 1827, 351-9.
Richard Welford, *Men of Mark 'Twixt Tyne and Tweed*, III, 1895, 188-90, 206-12.
GEC[okayne], *Complete Baronetage*, III, 1903, 261-2.
J A Venn, *Alumni Cantabrigienses*, part II (from 1752 to 1900), IV, 1951, 407, 437.
Elizabeth M Halcrow, "The Election Campaigns of Sir Charles Miles Lambert Monck," *Archaeologia Aeliana*, fourth series, XXXVI, 1958, 101-22.
F H W Sheppard [editor], *Survey of London*, XXXI, Part Two, 1963, 164.
The Victoria History of the Counties of England, *A History of Essex*, V, 1966, 193, and plate facing 248.
Sir Lewis Namier and John Brooke [editors], *The History of Parliament, The House of Commons 1754-1790*, 1985, 136-7.
R G Thorne [editor], *The History of Parliament, The House of Commons 1790-1820*, 1986, 610-12.